The *Art* of
Encouragement

Ray W. Lincoln

P-Book ISBN: 978-0-9996349-2-9

Apex Publications

Ingram, TX

© 2006, printed in New Zealand
© 2010, printed in the United States of America
© 2019, printed in the United States of America

DEDICATION

To the encouragers who, though
unaware, have lifted me so often
and may never have known that
they were angels in disguise.

*"Each helps the other and says to
his brother, 'Be strong,' the
craftsman encourages the goldsmith
…and spurs on him who strikes the
anvil."*
Isaiah 41:6-7

Acknowledgments

A book is seldom the work of one person. Yet one person usually gets all the credit. This injustice should always be corrected — hence the acknowledgements.

The Art of Encouragement is the result of years of help that people have given me and countless hours spent in developing the art with the aid of the unsuspecting contributors to this book — those I counseled and coached. I have learned so much from the people I have attempted to help. This book, then, is the result of too many people to name. Thank you.

Thanks to those who have recently encouraged me — among them some dear friends, David and Grace Petrie (who also aided in proofing the text), along with my wife, Mary Jo, who encouragingly worked by my side. David brings the steadying wisdom of a teacher who, by occupation, becomes a student of human nature and an encourager and developer of those in tender years. He also exudes the pleasure of thoughtful humor. Grace is all that her name indicates, with much talent packaged in a well-balanced personality. Both Mary Jo and I are deeply grateful for having them venture into our lives.

Now, thanks to you, the reader, for allowing me to, in some small way, help develop your gift of encouragement.

Ray W. Lincoln

Introduction

How to Use the Gift of Encouragement

Within these pages I have tried to cover some of the main points that should help those who are practicing the art of encouragement.

There are a few rules (science) for the task and these can be readily learned. The great rewards of seeing a person restored to health and happiness is, however, the more common joy of those who practice the skills of the encourager just as an artist would practice with paint and brush to obtain the desired effect. Develop your skills.

Help is inside you. The Holy Spirit, who indwells the followers of Jesus, speaks in the heart of the one you are trying to help at the same time that He speaks to you and through you. Never lose sight of this Divine partnership or you will lose your most effective edge.

To form a framework for my remarks, I have chosen to examine, in both English and Greek, the words commonly used for encouragement and to comment on their meaning and usage. It is to be hoped that this will not be too academic. I trust you will find it informative and a new slant on an age-old labor of love.

This book is meant to be read and reread, studied and digested. As you might expect, it won't read like a novel, but novels don't often educate, either.

My prayer is that you become an indispensable part of the lives of the people you love and serve. Your skilled understanding and application of encouragement and your cooperative work with the Holy Spirit of God, the Great Comforter, will equip you.

A brief checklist, which follows our examination of the "art," offers a map on which to plan your help.

One final thought: Not only will this booklet help those who are engaged in the task of being encouragers, but it will also help those who want to help themselves.

God bless.

Contents

The Art of Encouragement

The Approach of a Biblical Psychology

Comfort, yes, comfort my people, says the Lord.
~ Isaiah 40:1

Encourage the faint hearted.
~ I Thessalonians 5:14.

Want to be a great encourager?
You should then consider this: Air, shelter, food and encouragement are the basic necessities of life.

Surprised about encouragement?
Without air, shelter and food, we die. Without encouragement, the human spirit is likely to wither in the scorching heat of life's adversities or tire in the chase of life's goals. So it earns its place among the essentials.

You are desperately needed.
The demand is greater than the supply. Is there a soul wandering the face of this globe who doesn't need

encouragement? Not in reality; but some think they don't. Aren't they simply deceived? Yes, and at times not willing to admit their need of encouragement because of the risk of appearing to be weak or less than self-sufficient — as though self-sufficiency were a virtue.

However, such an attitude is not altogether bad because we need that appearance of strength at times. It can be the only thing that stands between us and the loss of self-respect. Jesus seldom punctured the delicate bubble of self-respect with which we hang onto our dignity. He found ways to encourage people that also lifted their self-esteem.

You will always be in demand and desperately needed if, when you both lift people as you help them, you also protect their dignity in the process.

Your confidence is needed — vicariously, that is.

Do you long to be an encourager, a doctor of the soul, soothing the pains and aches of more than flesh? Do you want to lift the brokenhearted, cure many an attack of depression, and strengthen the strong for yet more bold exploits? Then you will need a certain kind of understanding, a gentle spirit, a believable massage administered with the skilled touch of a confident, patient, repeated application that is always applied with confidence! You wouldn't want a medical doctor who was not sure of his diagnosis, would you?

2

Your confidence in the way you administer help goes a long way to instill confidence in others. Crushed people feed off the confidence of others. Confidence is also bolstered by prayer that further nurtures a struggling faith. However, since encouragement is the ointment for wounded and tired spirits and for those that would continue their struggle up the dizzy heights of achievement, a dose of its essential ingredients will soon take effect when persistently and confidently applied. People need your <u>confident</u> help.

Confidence is achieved by an unswerving faith in the God whose message you deliver.

Your learned skills are needed, so...

LEARN THE SKILL OF IMPLANTING COURAGE!

Words are usually coined to meet the need for more adequate communication. So let's start by examining some of these words we have coined in English to describe encouragement. As we become familiar with them, we will discover the skills we need. We will limit ourselves to two languages: English and Greek.

Ways to Give Them a Reason to Be Courageous

The word encouragement is made up of two words: "en" (which is another way of saying "in") and the word "courage." Together they mean to put courage into someone. That's really all it is: giving someone a reason to be courageous. If you lose sight of this you will have effectively killed your ability to help.

> # Simply put, encouragement instills courage.
>
> ✳

Emotional reasons instill courage

The reasoning we use to put courage into people's hearts isn't limited to the mental logic we call rational reasoning. It is more often the logic of emotion that we use. An emotional reason that persuades the mind and warms it at the same time often surpasses the cold facts of logic. Only sudden success can instill courage more efficiently than the warmth of an emotional reason.

Reasons like: "We love you and need you and want you to hold on!" Like: "I know you can do it. I believe in you!" These emotions of love and trust warm the coldness of their felt isolation. Think up your own phrases that use emotions to build courage. The stronger the emotion (if it is relevant to the occasion), the better the result.

4

To discover the emotion that will heal, ask yourself, "What is hurting them most or what do they passionately long for?" Then fashion your words to bolster hope and faith in the fulfillment of their need.

Mentally walk through their valley in their shoes. The identity of the emotional help you are looking for will soon become obvious to you when you do.

Understanding the different temperaments and targeting your remarks to the needs and preferences of their temperament is a distinct advantage. To gain an initial understanding of temperament theory and how God has made us read my book, INNERKINETICS — Your Blueprint to Excellence and Happiness. *It reveals the strengths of the adult and aids in their development to a life of fulfillment. For the parent or grandparent, read my parenting guides,* I'M A KEEPER *and* I'M STILL A KEEPER.. *Understanding yourself, your child, and the interactions between your temperaments will provide the guide you have sought to help you to parent with love and confidence.*

Visible Concern

We get to the heart through the mind. The mind registers both reason and emotion. Therefore, use all applicable avenues that the mind is equipped to monitor to reach the heart — sight, hearing, touch, etc. The sight of your concern and care, and the words you write or speak, along with your physical touch (where appropriate), can also be a part of effective communication. Without a lesson in propriety, let's simply say that all must be appropriate and proper. I must confess that the loving touch of my wife when she seeks to encourage me is a powerful message straight to my heart — one I should heed more!

Jesus stood by the grave of Lazarus and wept. His emotion, clearly seen by all, is the only element in the story that is warm. Seeing is convincing. In this miraculous reversal of death, He blends both faith and love in a touching moment of Divine care. The lesson for us is, even when we can't produce the needed miracle, we can at least show the love. Consider the healing powers of visible respect and love. Jesus did not underrate them in His ministry.

Emotional Words

We just spoke of emotion that is visible. Now let's focus on emotions that are conveyed by the audible channel. Words powered by emotions will more readily enter and find the heart than just words. The emotion is st conveyed as a "felt" love, and it is discernible in the human voice. We call it intonation. The right tone of voice conveys a meaning just as certainly as the word itself. The way to get the right tone in your voice is to <u>live your love</u> in front of them. Even poorly chosen words can sometimes be forgiven when they are spoken in a tone of love. Therefore, learn to speak with emotional content and increase your effectiveness. Speak not only <u>from</u> your heart but <u>with</u> your heart. Feel inside of you the words you speak. An encourager without warmth is suspected of a lack of empathy.

The power of a word also depends on its appropriateness. Choose the right word. Increase your skills by expanding your vocabulary. Most often the right word is the simple one that is commonly used and fully understood as long as it is communicating the correct thought. However, the choice of word is so much more than "the one with the right meaning."

Every word has an emotive content — that is, it conveys a feeling. For example, calling a person "you" does not create the same feeling as calling them by name, "Angela." Saying one must go and talk with so-and-so conveys a different emotion from saying you must hurry and talk to them. Words like love, lust, longing, like, want, and desire all have different emotions and register different emotional levels. Choose your words for both their meaning and their emotive power. Use a word with the right meaning, the right emotion, and the one with the right strength of emotion. Skills are sharpened when you pay attention to the details!

Let's remind ourselves: Caring is a divine emotion and we all use it at times because we were created in the image of God. Therefore, we can access it naturally. It's also older than we are and wiser than all our words.

Remember, our lifestyle as followers of Jesus is to never forget the power and wisdom He brings to our lives. Therefore, pray for His help and rely on His aid as you encourage others. If you don't, what in the world are you thinking? We should never work alone as comforters. We are promised the aid of the Comforter Himself. We should recognize our need of God's inspiration and wisdom.

However, don't rely on God and then fail to labor to increase your skills and your gifts. Someone once said, "Pray as though everything depends on God and work as though it all depends on you." It's not the best theology, but it gets the point across.

What we can't do is touch their spirit in the loving way God touches spirits. We will touch their spirit, but the touch is clumsy in comparison to God's touch. The perfect act of encouragement occurs when we minister to their need with wisdom and love and God reaches into their spirits as well. Then they feel something that surpasses all the feelings they have experienced before. Their healing is whole and complete. They are new creatures in Christ Jesus, regenerated by His Spirit. The touch of God is His loving miracle.

Build Determination

Encouragers often quit before their task is completed. They comfort and soothe and lift a person out of their depressed condition only to think that is all encouragers are called to do. A person saved from the ravages of destructive gloom must not only return to health but must gain strength to withstand future attacks. Determination and perseverance build the muscles of our human spirits and strengthens us for future trials. Build determination in them by the determination they see in you.

We often think of the human spirit as being weak and fragile, probably because of its bodiless state. However, the human spirit is the strongest "muscle" in our systems. We can't afford for failure or despair to weaken the human spirit — hence, the importance of completing the task of reconstruction. A word I like better than reconstruction is "re-creation." We are re-created when we are led from doubt to faith, when we are lifted from despair to hope. It is a journey back into the image of God again. God is confident and persistent, and we must be, too.

The happy blending of self-confidence and God confidence is found in the words of Paul:

> **"I can do all things through Christ who strengthens me." ~Philippians 4: 13.**

Don't leave your post until the one you are helping is able to voice these words with inner comfort. Confidence will come after they are feeling comfortable with saying these words. Only then will they look and feel like the image of God has been stamped on their spirit.

Display your confidence in them. You have every reason to do so. The Holy Spirit is working with you and failure is not a word He feels comfortable with. You will succeed, and they will succeed, if you follow the pattern of biblical psychology and trust in God.

> *For those who are unfamiliar with the term "biblical psychology," here is a simple definition: If we can find it as a teaching in the Bible, it is biblical. If it has to do with human behavior, it is human psychology. Put the two together and you get "biblical psychology." It is what the Bible teaches about human behavior.*

When we know that others are depending on us and believing in us, we are prone to rise to the challenge, square our shoulders, and face our circumstances defiantly. Your goal is to build this determination in them by your determination and your faith in God.

An odd lesson

What I find so odd is that it took so long for the English-speaking people to coin the word *encourage*. It wasn't until 1450AD that the first use of the word is recorded.

One other noteworthy fact is that, although English words often change their meaning faster than we can get used to them, this word has not changed the meaning of the word encourage since it was coined. That's testimony to its adequacy and the persistence of the human need for courage.

Approaches from the Greeks

"To Take Heart"

As the ancient Greeks coined their words for courage and encouragement, they apparently (if we are to judge by this word's prolific use) found the meaning "to take heart" most useful. In a nation that bore the Spartans and the armies of Alexander the Great, to "take heart" must also have been a required national trait.

The Greek word *tharreo*, "to take heart," translates into Greek such Old Testament Hebrew phrases as "fear not" and "don't be afraid." It was also used in the New Testament to record these same phrases from the lips of the greatest encourager of all, Jesus.

Overcoming Fear

Jesus was in the habit of beginning His help with the words, "Do not be afraid." He seemed to want to dispel fear as though it was impossible for Him to proceed in its presence. Fear was dealt with before help and healing were attempted. There's a powerful lesson here.

Fear downsizes us and actively opposes the forces of courage and confidence in our minds. Courage restores us so that we reflect the awesome image of God. That's far more than the Greeks originally had in mind when they used the word, but it's the foundation of biblical psychology. Courage is much more powerful than fear. If you would be an encourager, you must believe this and be seen to believe it!

In the early chapters of the book of Acts, the disciples exhibit great courage that is seen by the onlookers as boldness. A careful reading of these chapters will show that their boldness played a large part in their winning the people of their day to faith in the resurrection of Jesus. It was also this boldness that defeated their own feelings of fear since they were putting their lives at risk by talking openly about Jesus and His resurrection. When courage is entrenched in a human mind, fear has little foothold and slides down its own slippery slope, while courage wins great victories.

Always be aware of the proximity of fear and its likely victory over a despairing, despondent soul. Exorcise it by replacing it with faith and trust in God. Do not ignore it if you detect its presence. Follow the pattern of Jesus, and deal with it first. However, the treatment for the displacing of fear is the same treatment for the lifting of the spirit. The only difference is that fear needs to be identified and admitted before we can face it and do something about it.

Whatever you do, do not be judgmental of a person who is afraid, because no encourager can claim to be free from fear's assaults, and an attitude of judgment is a sure turn-off. Empathetically lead a person away from fear's clutches, saying to yourself, "But for the grace of God there go I." In all encouragement, it makes sense to minor on the negative (fear) and major on the positive (courage).

Courage is a mental attitude. It is thinking like God thinks when faced with fear's destructive forces. God thinks only of winning the battle. He faces impossible odds with confidence. When He created the world, He faced a task too big for us to even contemplate in our little minds. For God, the fear of failure was ever lurking in the shadows because He had no materials to even begin with and had never done this before. His thinking dismissed the thoughts of failure as though those thoughts were the impossible and he courageously attacked the making of a universe out of nothing. That's the kind of thinking to instill in the mind of struggling humans. We must act like God if we are to win and crush the negative forces of our own impossibilities.

To be an effective encourager, we must display the courage that is embedded in our own faith, thus setting the mood for its resurrection in the heart of the one who is afraid.

Love Builds Courage Muscles
The renewed image of God in us, which Jesus called the abundant life, is built on displacing fear with love. Remember what John said in his first letter, *"Perfect love casts out fear,"* I John 4:18. Encouragers are experts, using their weapon of love to drive out the demon of fear from the hearts of people attacked by the evil one.

Then, you — the encourager and victor over the dark pits of despair — calmly point the way to faith. John gives us both of our tools. He also says, *"Faith is the victory that overcomes the world"* and all its valleys of despair. Our plan is simple. Exhibit love and instill faith!

When we have instilled courage and driven out the demon of fear, Jesus reminds us that it will leave a vacuum. The vacuum is then filled with even more demons if we don't fill it with something else. Therefore, as encouragers, we mustn't feel that loving people is all we have to do. As the demon of fear leaves, fill the vacuum created by the absence of fear with faith.

Presence Intimidates Fear

Encouraging people to take heart is not all a matter of what we <u>do</u>. Encouragers all too often forget the influence of presence — *their* presence — which for disciples of Jesus is a presence infused with the presence of the Holy Spirit. Remember, again, the close connection between who <u>we</u> are (encouragers) and who <u>the Holy Spirit</u> is (the comforter). Our ministry (as encouragers) and the Holy Spirit's ministry are one ministry. We never encourage without there being two of us working together at the same task.

Presence affects all of us. A person walks on the stage and exhibits a "presence." We all know how powerful that can be and how instrumental it is to the actor's performance. A counselor sits in front of another person and is something more than a counselor. He (or she) emits a presence, an aura, that the other person can feel. That presence, unfortunately, is sometimes a nervous presence or a self-confessed apology for trying to help. I've even heard a counselor say they will do their best to *try* to help, with a heavy emphasis on the word

14

"try." Pity the despairing one. They already are having their worst fears realized, and that is that no one will probably be able to help them — including this counselor.

Wake up, encourager! God is with you! You are equipped with all the wisdom, power, and ability of the Holy Spirit. Or don't you believe that? The Holy Spirit is not going to hide or apologize for His presence or His promises, and it will be very evident whether you share His confidence or not. Please, if you don't believe with all your heart that the Holy Spirit is going to work through you, don't spread your contagious germs of doubt all over someone who is already depressed. They don't need that. Nor does the Holy Spirit benefit from your help.

The need is for someone who believes God to sit in front of them or alongside them with the absolute confidence that all the help of God Almighty is theirs, and that they come in His name and with His Spirit. People will take heart when they feel the presence of God!

The healing power of upbeat confidence within the encourager has, at times, been all that was needed for the lifting of a sunken soul. The bearer of hope has an aura of expectation and healing around them that is, in itself, an ingredient of their curative balm.

Be conscious of "being" as well as "doing." Don't underestimate the effect of your presence and the presence of the Heavenly Occupant of your spirit.

An encourager who doesn't give the impression of being someone special is a failure before they begin. You must be positive and full of faith before you can be full of the Holy Spirit.

The Greek word "to take heart" is, I believe, a wonderful image of what we are about. It is, of course, the choice of the New Testament writers.

"To Exhort"

Stand With

Another Greek word, *parakaleo*, is often used in the sense of "to exhort." It occurs frequently in words of encouragement to soldiers and in the exhortations of the commander who is about to go with his troops into the jaws of danger. This word creates the image of someone standing alongside someone else and calling them to engage the enemy together.

What a picture! As an encourager, you are called to stand alongside the one you are encouraging, not at a "professional distance." Professionalism is not always the mood we want to convey. It can be, at times, cold and ineffective in matters that concern wounded emotions and depreciated self-images.

Encouragement involves a personal commitment to the one you would help. Stand with them, feeling their pain (both empathy and sympathy, where needed), and act in the same way you would appreciate if they were encouraging you.

An encourager doesn't position himself as superior either, but as a fellow pilgrim who tastes the same fears and whose knees shake at the same prospects, but whose heart is courageous.

Encouragement Leads to Comforting. What's the Difference, If Any?

It's only a short step from encouragement to comfort. In fact, the encourager cannot divorce the two. We are, therefore, not surprised to find this Greek word for exhorting also used for comforting the sad and fearful. I want to suggest you view your ministry of encouragement as a ministry of comforting. This slight change in our thinking can often bring out of us a more caring, Christlike spirit, unnoticed by us but obvious to the hurting heart.

Does Admonishing Have a Place in this Ministry?

The use of this Greek word, *parakaleo,* will teach us something else of importance. It carries the imperative element of the closely related task of admonishing. Gentle admonition is sometimes the task of the encourager. However, the warm, consoling nature of the word is never absent, and the gentleness of the admonition is the secret of its success.

Plato taught the need to give moral and rational admonition. His stance was: If reason (*sophronizein*) did not prevail to bring the grieving one to their senses, then to discipline (*paideuein*) them was the only remaining logical alternative. The ancient world, lacking the grace and love of Christ, had to resort in the long run to a firm handling of the grieving and depressed to hold together the fragmenting life of a society that had no final answer to human failing except human effort and discipline.

Thank God, we have a God of love, forgiveness, and tender compassion to turn to for real life affirming help. Severe discipline in the face of failure is not the Christian way, so we divorce ourselves from Plato's use of force. Our biblical psychology leads us to the uplifting of the broken and the failing, and to the restoration of their lives in love.

The only helpful point I would extract from non-biblical antiquity on this issue is that it is (as they taught), in the final analysis, useless and damaging to continue lamenting and bemoaning your condition, because that leads to self-pity and all the destructive factors of negativity. The biblical teaching that counters this state of negative mental health is in the much misunderstood word "repent" (change the way you think about it) and in embracing the healing warmth of God's total forgiveness and uplifting love.

An interesting fact also emerges from non-biblical antiquity: the practice of inscribing (on the stones set up for the dead) words supposedly from the dead person, exhorting the living to stop lamenting. Even the dead, they taught, were telling them to stop grieving, while having no real basis for a hope like ours. Aren't we glad we have hope from the one who has conquered death and shown us the secrets of a perfect life!

The encourager who follows in the steps of Jesus has something to offer that no other belief, discipline or psychological theory possesses. We offer the true encouragement of God, the solace of prayer (a direct, anytime, as-needed, two-way, heart-to-heart communication with God); the power of a faith grounded in an infinite loving and able person; a love that surpasses all understanding; a hope that is real; and a trust in the God who holds us in His hands and who has not yet said His last words or finished working in everything that happens to us for our good. *"God is wonderful in counsel and excellent in guidance,"* Isaiah 28:29. Trust in God and be amazed at how your feelings are transformed.

There is a sense in which we ought to console and encourage ourselves without dependence on an encourager. Therefore, while encouraging a person, teach them at the same time how to console and encourage themselves. To use a well-grasped analogy: don't just feed them fish; teach them to fish. Teach them to feed the needs of their own spirit by overcoming negativism and evil with the positive and the good, *"Overcome evil with good,"* Romans 12:21.

The Wisdom of Common Sense

Treatments for the discouraged and depressed offered by people who don't seek the help of God are both good treatments and not-so-good treatments. Among the good ideas that surround the use of this word ("to exhort") in ancient Greece are these: getting some much needed rest, the soothing effects of music, and rational reasoning, which shows the futile nature of negative thinking patterns. Often, the human help that is offered is sound. However, help that stops short of what God can do is always, in my book, incomplete.

19

I want to offer you something from the creative hand of God that I have found effective. Create a diversion. Change the environment. By that I mean, take a person who is battered and weary of heart out for a walk in God's impressive world or for coffee and a walk to a favorite place, and let the influences of everything around you help to heal the moment and relax the spirit. Let the magnificence of God's creation and its wonder enter their spirit. Not only will they hear your words more sympathetically, but God's inner voice as well. Doing so has been the breakthrough in many stubborn cases for me. Try it.

Confidence

We have pointed to the fact that confidence creates courage. They are siblings born of the same faith. Confidence builders like the following can, and do, help:

"You can do it!"

"With God, nothing is impossible."

"I've always thought of you as a winner. This is another chance for me to believe in you."

"What God started in you, He will finish."

"You're my hero and you're proving it to me again!"

Here's a well kept secret, barely hidden in the word confidence: Can you see the word "confide" in confidence?

To confide is to tell someone a secret or simply to tell them how you feel. Gently telling a person your believable feelings about them certainly will help build their confidence. However, confidence is built over time, so wait patiently for your caring love to work its magic.

I don't want you to underrate the power of repetition as a powerful tool either, so let me raise its importance again. Constantly dripping water wears away the stone, remember. Repeated attempts at building confidence in a sports person is a tried and proven method found in a coach's arsenal, and it's not age sensitive. All ages rise to the positive power of repeated attempts to encourage. Practice the power of perpetually pumping up people! Don't shy away from such a simple positive act since it does not oppose biblical truth and is innate in acts of love and faith-building.

Is It Wrong to Believe in Yourself?

Here's another step in our understanding as encouragers. Confidence is having a belief. Beliefs are the reasons we attempt to do things. They lie behind every accomplishment as the motivating power.

Therefore, encouragers are people who help other people believe in something. "In themselves? In hidden powers? In God? In the encourager? In what?" you ask.

As long as a belief is there, we can be motivated; but the object of our belief is a factor in determining the <u>power</u> that is created by that belief. If I believe that my cat is in the room with me, my motivation to leave is nil. I don't fear my cat; I'll stay. If I believe a tiger is in the room with me, my motivation to leave is at fever pitch! The object of our belief has a lot to do with the nature and power of our motivation.

Likewise, if I believe in my encourager or myself, my motivation is strong enough to make a difference to my mental state. But if I also believe in God's power in me, my motivation is even greater.

It is not wrong to believe in yourself, but it is less effective than believing in God as well.

Self-Confidence and God Confidence — Together They Are the Ultimate

Self-confidence empowers. But a God-confidence, coupled with a belief in ourselves, is the ultimate. Paul said it best, *"I can do all things through Christ who strengthens me," Philippians 4:13.* Two things are placed side-by-side in that verse: self-confidence ("I can") and God-confidence are not alternatives between which we must choose. God's strength in us boosts our self-confidence. When we let it play its part in our confidence, we say with increased confidence, "I can!" The greatest self-confidence is built with God-confidence. Therefore, to say we should be confident in God but not in ourselves is simply not to understand the relationship between our human systems and the way God's inner presence works in us. Note carefully the essential emphasis of the two in Paul's words, *"I can do all things through Christ who strengthens me."*

Here is another reason why self-confidence and God-confidence go together. The ability to control ourselves (self-control) is the fruit of the Holy Spirit in our lives. Self-control depends on self-motivation, and that in turn depends on self-belief.

There is no motivation without belief. God wants us to live in the confidence and belief that being created in His image, we are capable creatures. This fact is true of all humans, as we see from the astounding feats of success achieved by people with no belief in God. In fact, we can reflect His image and demonstrate the truth of our being created in God's image even if we don't believe in Him. Unwilling witnesses to our origin in God are all around us, but witnesses they are. And don't forget, all this is doubly possible in Christ. Hence Paul's claim in Philippians 4:13.

Find the Motivating Reason for Lack of Self-Confidence.

People who don't believe in themselves have a reason why they don't believe in themselves, just as people who don't believe in God have a reason why they don't believe in God. It is usually a reason strongly colored by their emotions, no matter how academically they present their position. A skilled encourager *gently* (please note the constant reference to gentleness) probes the person's emotional history — recent

---

> ## To put courage in someone's heart is to build his confidence.

---

or long buried — and finds that emotionally charged reason. You may have to walk in their shoes a little and feel their heartbeat before you find it. Once the reason surfaces, we can approach and defuse it. Encouragers should pray for guidance when entering the sometimes private territory of another's emotions to help them around or over their mountain of difficulty. Where there is a blockage to healthy confidence, it must be removed if real help is going to be given.

25

The Encouragement of God's Word

"God's Word is a comfort in times of trouble," says Psalm 119:50. Nothing encourages more than the Word of God resurrected from the memory and applied to the heart of one who believes. The reason has already been explained. Belief is the motivating factor of life; and belief in God's own words is the supreme motivation. Be equipped with words such as:

> Look at the birds of the air; they do not sow or reap or store away in barns, and yet your heavenly Father feeds them. Are you not much more valuable than they?...And why do you worry about clothes? See how the lilies of the field grow. They do not labour or spin. Yet I tell you that not even Solomon in all his splendor was dressed like one of these...But seek first his kingdom and his righteousness, and all these things will be given to you as well. ~Matthew 6:26, 28-30, 33

> I have seen his ways and will heal him; I will also lead him, and restore comforts to him. ~Isaiah 57: 18.

> If you have any encouragement from being united with Christ, if any comfort from his love, if any fellowship with the Spirit, if any tenderness and compassion, then make my joy complete by being

like-minded, having the same love, being one in spirit and purpose. ~Philippians 2:1

This refers to an encouragement of love and identifies it with the mind of Christ. How encouraging for the encourager!

Encouragement Is a Creative Art

As in all matters where we partner with God, creativity is expected on our part. Are we not acting in the image of God the creator when we are creative? The excellent encourager has learned that encouraging is an exercise in creativity.

Think of ways that will make you more effective, and in your creativity — as in all partnerships with God, —discern what God's Spirit is doing and has already said in the mind of the discouraged one. Then, follow His lead. How do I find that out? Conversation, attentive listening, and prayer (in which you ask for God's lead and expect the answer) will be your compass and your chart.

Encouragement will never go out of style! If it is your passion in life to encourage others, you will never be without a job.

Checklist for the Encourager

- Have you prayed?
- Is your spirit in an attitude of dependence on God's help and not in the clutches of some unhelpful attitude?
- Approach the person in need with confidence.
- Listen very carefully — not just for the main plot of their story but to the subplots that lead you to the motivations you seek.
- Is there a real fear at work? If so, discover what it is and deal with it.
- Let your love be obvious.
- Build faith and confidence.
- Follow the lead of God's Spirit.
- Lift the person. Always leave them lifted. Lift them into the hands of God!

Appendix

REAL HELP FOR THE DEPRESSED

Since depression is as easy to "catch" as the common cold, here is help from above for the depressed.

To discover that God wants to say something to us when we are depressed is in itself encouraging. His encouraging words are better than any other human's help. However, to feel that encouragement we must believe him! Belief starts in the mind — in the way we think!

Read the following verses and ask the one you are seeking to help to indicate the verses that speak most to them and to repeat those verses daily until the cloud of depression leaves and the sun begins to shine again.

Think Differently – Try Believing These Words from God.

Fear not for I am with you; be not dismayed, for I am your God. I will strengthen you, yes, I will help you. ~Isaiah 41:10. **(Believe God's promise to you.)**

...the ransomed of the Lord... shall obtain joy and gladness, and sorrow and sighing shall flee away. ~Isaiah 51:11. **(Hope is on the horizon! Believe it.)**

When you pass through the waters, I will be with you; and through the rivers they shall not overthrow you. When you walk through the fire, you shall not be burned, nor shall the flame scorch you. ~Isaiah 43:2. **(This depression of yours will not harm you if you daily trust God as you pass through its murky waters.)**

He heals the broken hearted and binds up their wounds. ~Psalm 147:3. ~ **(That inner wound is healed by faith in the Great Physician. Believe God is healing it — now.)**

The eyes of the Lord are on the righteous, and His ears are open to their cry. The righteous cry out, and the Lord hears, and delivers them out of all their troubles. ~Psalm 34:15-17. **(As you believe all will be well, God will lead you out of your troubles. A cry to God for help is never unheeded, but don't sit down and give up. Keep walking through the trouble.)**

I will not forget you. ~Isaiah 49:15. **(His eye is on you all the time. Believe this and let it soak into your soul.)**

Joy comes in the morning. ~Psalm 30:5. ***(Hope!)***

Happy is the man who trusts in the Lord, and whose hope is in the Lord. ~Jeremiah 17:7. ***(We have an advantage over those who don't believe in God. Happiness is found in our faith in God.)***

According to your faith it will be done to you. ~Matthew 9:29. ***(Your faith heals you. It's the way we are made. Strong faith is needed for a fast recovery.)***

For I am persuaded that neither death nor life, nor angels nor principalities nor powers, nor things present nor things to come, nor height nor depth, nor any other created thing, shall be able to separate us from the love of God which is in Christ Jesus our Lord. ~Romans 8:38-39. ***(Our relationship is safe. God will never stop loving us.)***

Likewise, the Spirit also helps in our weaknesses. For we do not know what we should pray for as we ought, but the Spirit Himself makes intercession for us with groanings which cannot be uttered. ~Romans 8:26. ***(Don't know what you want? Don't know what to pray? Never mind, God's got that covered, too.)***

Finally, brethren, whatever things are true, noble, just, pure, lovely, of good report, if there is any virtue and if there is anything praiseworthy — meditate on these things. ~Philippians 4:8. **(Here's our thought pattern. The ONLY WAY out of our depression is the path of positive thoughts.)**

Therefore do not worry, saying "What shall we eat? or What shall we drink? or What shall we wear?"... For your heavenly Father knows that you need all these things. ~Matthew 6:31-32. **(Anxiety can be a potent factor in your depression. If you can believe that God will take care of you and your needs, while of course you do all that you can do, the demon of anxiety can be slain.)**

I will never leave you nor forsake you. ~Hebrews 13:5. **(Loneliness lives in the pit of despair. Make God your companion whenever you visit the pit. He keeps His promise. We have to believe it. That's all!)**

Be strong and of good courage, do not fear nor be afraid... for the Lord Your God... goes with you. ~Deuteronomy 31:6. **(Fear is another common factor in depression. Belief brings courage, so believe that God goes with you everywhere!)**

Cast your burden on the Lord. ~Psalm 55:22. **(Depression is caused by burdens, stresses that we carry. But why carry them if God will? Have faith in God's promises!)**

For God has not given us the spirit of fear, but of power and of love and of a sound mind. ~2 Timothy 1:7 **(For the depressed, a sound mind is the challenge. A sound mind is a mind full of faith and positive thoughts. Believe God and this is your gift.)**

The Lord is my helper; I will not fear. What can man do to me? ~Hebrews 13:6 **(Afraid of someone and what they can do? They are nothing compared to God.)**

Do not be afraid of sudden terror… for the Lord will be your confidence. ~Proverbs 3:25-26. **(We have reason to be calm.)**

You will keep him in perfect peace whose mind is stayed on You, because he trusts in You. ~Isaiah 26:3. **(The way out of depression is in controlling your mind. Keep your mind on God, not on yourself or your worries. There's no higher help.)**

Books by Ray W. Lincoln

If you prefer to read books that get right to the heart of the matter, you will find them in this list. The goal in producing these monographs is to provide immediate help in an easy-to-read and quick-to assimilate format. The topics were chosen from help most often sought from Dr. Lincoln by his clients, friends, and church members where he was pastor. More books are on the way! So stay in touch!

Finding God's Will for You — How can I know what God wants me to do and be? Ray Lincoln has been asked this question countless times over his forty-plus years of ministry. Here he guides his readers through fundamental steps to determining God's will and obtaining the peace of confident faith.

Path to Positive Internal Power — Self-esteem is the current topic of hundreds of books available these days. This guide and workbook directs the reader to improved self-esteem and gives guidance for building self-esteem in children and teens.

Personal Excellence — Eleven principles to adopt from the life of Christ that will guide you to success in all your endeavors.

Willed in Heaven and Made to Work on Earth — What is the secret to a long and happy marriage? Herein is revealed the "real secret" that really is no secret at all. Using the example of the marriage of Mary and Joseph, which had all the elements to create failure, the author shows how God designed the marriage relationship to work.

"I love you," signed Jesus — the inspiring account of Christ's suffering as you have not heard it told before. First printed in New Zealand and "sold out," this scholarly study into the details of Christ's passion will stir you to love and serve the One who died that we might live.

The 4 Temperaments — A handy and compact reference for parents and a valuable tool in parenting the temperaments represented in their progeny. It contains detailed descriptions of the four temperaments and provides initial suggestions for how to parent each specifically.

I May Frustrate You, But I'm A Keeper! —When you truly understand how and why your children think and act the way they do, you can parent them to become the best they can be and live a life of fulfillment. Contrary to the thoughts of secular (and of many Christian) psychologists, we are not born with strengths *and weaknesses*. We are hard-wired with a temperament that reflects the image of God. God is not in the business of creating anything with a weakness. Your child was created with only strengths. So were you. Where did the weaknesses come from? This book will tell you. Understanding is underrated! This book will lead you to parent you child with understanding and confidence.

Available at **www.raywlincoln.com**

INNERKINETICS — Your Blueprint to Excellence and Happiness
This book is self-discovery with powerful new insights, the first book written on InnerKinetics®! Hundreds of people are finding these insights have changed their lives and dispelled myths like...

- Success is all about proven principles.
- Everyone has weaknesses, so all you can do is minimize them.
- I'm smart enough to find my own way to an exciting life by trial and error.

Available at **www.raywlincoln.com**.

* 9 7 8 0 9 9 9 6 3 4 9 2 9 *